But Stage C, when prizes are awarded, depends on the luck of the Draw… on you.

YOU MUST RETURN YOUR NUMBERS TO ENTER THE DRAW.

And as you'll find out when they arrive, there's every reason for returning them promptly… because

THE SOONER YOU ENTER, THE MORE YOU COULD WIN!!!

So please be on the lookout for the special brown envelope from Prize Draw containing your numbers, and be ready to act the moment it arrives. Good luck!

Yours sincerely,

Sebastian Millionaire

Prize Draw Manager

P.S. If you come through Stage C as one of our 1,014 prize winners, I shall be in touch with you again. If you win the First Prize, I'd give you official confirmation of the good news right away: then we'd arrange for you to receive your cheque at a special reception. And off you'd go, the richer by AT LEAST £175,000!

RICHER BY £175,000!!!

5

NORDSOL FERIE

Torvegade 5 . 6950 Ringkøbing . Telex 60 906

Tlf. 97 32 25 11

WELCOME TO YOUR SUMMERHOUSE

Nordsol Ferie bit you, also in the name of your landlord,
welcome to your summerhouse.

We hope that you will have a happy stay with lots of sun
and many good experiences.

Please read the meter - WHITOUT DECIMALS - on your arrival
and departure. Please pay the amount at our office cn
your departure together with the key until 10.00 am.

Please notice that our service-chief after ended rental
will check the house, to value wether it is left in the
same condition as you recieved it in or not. If we find
that the house is not properly cleaned, we will have to
collect a suitable amount of money to cover the expenses
connected with cleaning up the house.

Please be aware that you on ordinary days will be able to
reach us at our office. Phone nr. 97 32 25 11 between
09.00 am to 05.00 pm.

Once again, WELCOME.

With kindly regards
Nordsol Ferie

Erik Lyhne Petersen

SOMMERHUSE OVERALT I DANMARK . Giro 8 04 04 51 . Telefax 97 32 06 88

6

Exploring Language

Exploring

Letters

An anthology of
everyday letters

RICHARD BAIN

CAMBRIDGE
UNIVERSITY PRESS

Published by the Press Syndicate of the University of Cambridge
The Pitt Building, Trumpington Street, Cambridge CB2 1RP
40 West 20th Street, New York, NY 10011–4211, USA
10 Stamford Road, Oakleigh, Melbourne 3166, Australia

Photography by Graham Portlock

© Cambridge University Press 1993

First published 1993

Printed in Great Britain at the University Press, Cambridge.

A catalogue record for this book is available from the British Library.

ISBN 0 521 44625 2 paperback

Acknowledgements

Thanks are due to the following for permission to reproduce from copyright material:

Page 8, reproduced by permission of Anne Coppen; page 12, reproduced by permission of D. B. Roberts & Partners; pages 17–20, letters reproduced by permission of the *Newcastle Evening Chronicle* and the *Early Times*; page 21, extract from *Boy* by Roald Dahl, reproduced by permission of the publishers Jonathan Cape Limited and Penguin Books Limited; page 22, extract from *A Pack of Liars* by Anne Fine © 1988, reproduced by permission of Hamish Hamilton Ltd.

Every effort has been made to reach copyright holders. The publishers would be glad to hear from anyone whose rights they have unknowingly infringed.

Contents

*The purpose of this book is to encourage you to collect and explore letters for yourself.
Please don't just rely on the letters in this book.*

CASHCOUNT

**The Prize Draw Association Limited,
St. John's House,
Smithson Road,
Bedford MK45 5BW**

FROM THE PRIZE DRAW MANAGER
Reference: 8885612777 401757 4880

27 New Street
Herthington
East Stourside
ES9 7SA

Dear Mr. Brown,
This is to advise you that in the latest Prize Draw, recently announced on television, your name has come through the first two stages in the Draw.

In Stage A, we asked our computer to tell us who in East Stourside should be invited to take part. When it came up with the list of participants in Herthington not only was New Street represented, it has picked the Brown household to receive six numbers, any of which could win you any of the 1,014 prizes – including a huge First Prize of £175,000.

YOU COULD WIN
FIRST PRIZE OF £175, 000

Stage B, the allocation of Prize Draw numbers, has just taken place. Your personal allocation of six numbers is on its way to you now, and should reach you within the next few days. You are therefore safely through two of the three stages that there are to becoming a winner.

MANAGER: JOHN B. JAMIESON

GENERAL INSURANCE LTD

Marshall House
Hampton Gardens
Bournemouth BH1 1JD

TELEPHONE: (0202) 095533
FAX (0202) 052899

```
MR. R. BROWN
27 NEW STREET
HERTHINGTON
EAST STOURSIDE
ES9 7SA
```

Your reference   Our reference 9026536H   Date 6thNovember 1990

Dear Sirs,

Re: Insured : Mr R Brown
Policy Number : PFO 1000
Loss Date : 14th October 1990

We acknowledge receipt of your recent communication.Repairs
may be authorised in accordance with the attached letter that
should be passed to the repairer named.
We await the fianl account.

Yours faithfully,

S PARSONS
CLAIMS DEPARTMENT

Member of **ABI**   Registered office
Hampton Garden
Bournemouth BH
Registered Num

Home Farm
Bailey's Lane
Northcombe,
Loundshire.
NB8 2DW

Jan 20th – 91

Dear Browns,

Thank you for the lovely ducks, which make a very handsome addition to the duck pool table. The little black one is very unusual. What a good job they don't all quack or squawk!

Glad you liked the book. (I liked it too!) Sounds as if you had a fine time in the cottage. Made a nice change for Christmas I should think. Do you remember you came to us for New Year once and there was a very heavy fall of snow? We walked round Lound in the middle of the road (deep drifts on both sides) with baby Andrew in a sling then you walked to Sutton crossroads on New Year's Eve with the Shelties and had to carry them back because they got ice between their toes.

We enjoyed ourselves - 8 for Christmas Dinner - then about 6 of us for 4 days. Emma and her new boy friend Dave, and Lucy drove down to London to see the New Year in, while Sally and Russ came to visit us

Our only exciting event is that my poor little car, safely parked at the side of the road outside college decided to catch fire for no apparent reason. The A level class and I were giving our attention to Richard II when a fire engine came up, making a dreadful racket. "Perhaps the house next door has caught fire," I said. "No. It's gone to a car." "Not a little grey one?" I thought they were having me on - - - - We are now waiting to hear from the Insurers. A write-off the garage thinks.

Went to see 'Rich II' at Stratford last week - a very laid-back, stiff production I thought. Didn't like Anton Lesser's Bolingbroke.

Inspection - week after next - but they seem to be v. interested in Business Studies, links with industry etc. Won't start another Sheet - Happy New Year Love to you all. Anne.

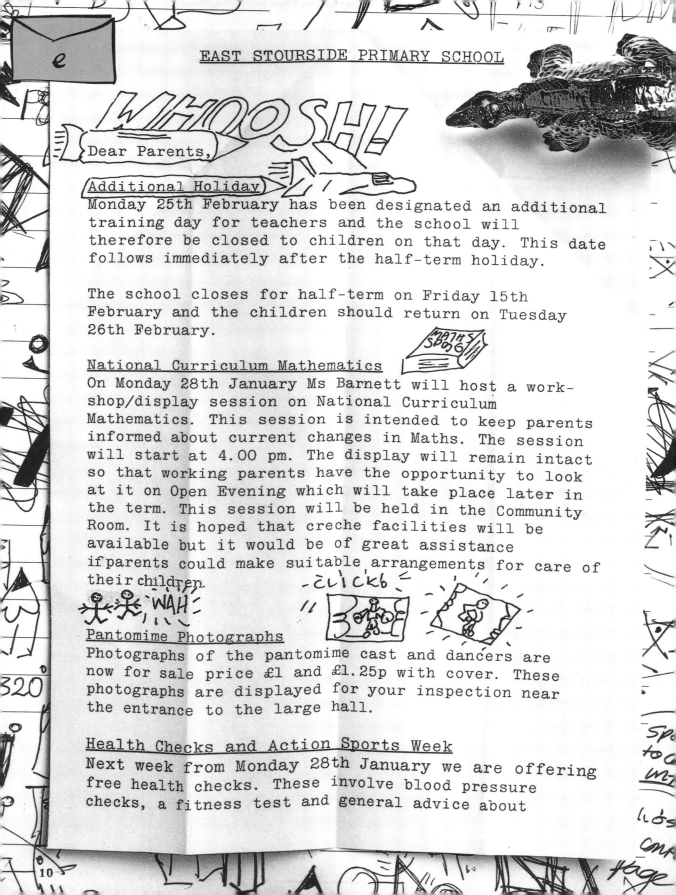

EAST STOURSIDE PRIMARY SCHOOL

WHOOSH!

Dear Parents,

Additional Holiday

Monday 25th February has been designated an additional training day for teachers and the school will therefore be closed to children on that day. This date follows immediately after the half-term holiday.

The school closes for half-term on Friday 15th February and the children should return on Tuesday 26th February.

National Curriculum Mathematics

On Monday 28th January Ms Barnett will host a workshop/display session on National Curriculum Mathematics. This session is intended to keep parents informed about current changes in Maths. The session will start at 4.00 pm. The display will remain intact so that working parents have the opportunity to look at it on Open Evening which will take place later in the term. This session will be held in the Community Room. It is hoped that creche facilities will be available but it would be of great assistance if parents could make suitable arrangements for care of their children.

Pantomime Photographs

Photographs of the pantomime cast and dancers are now for sale price £1 and £1.25p with cover. These photographs are displayed for your inspection near the entrance to the large hall.

Health Checks and Action Sports Week

Next week from Monday 28th January we are offering free health checks. These involve blood pressure checks, a fitness test and general advice about weight, diet, smoking, etc. These health checks are available free in the Community Room and are carried out by the Community Health Group.

At the same time the Action Sports Group will be in school offering practical advice on improving your fitness for all ages no matter what your current physical condition (fit or not!). The school has set up an exercise room and this facility will be available from next week for use by those parents and community members who are eager to improve or sustain their fitness level. See the Community Notice Board for further details.

Cars in the Yard
Please refrain from bringing cars into the school yard as this is an obvious source of danger to children.

Parents and Friends Group
Parents and Friends are starting a new term of fund raising events.

If you have any odd balls of wool or material you can send into school they would be appreciated.

Yours sincerely,

Mrs S. Robinson

Mrs. S. Robinson
Headteacher
23.1.92

D. B. Roberts & Partners

D.B. Roberts FSVA ARVA W.R. Brookes FSVA K.E.H. Crown FNAEA

**ESTATE AGENTS
VALUERS
AUCTIONEERS
SURVEYORS**

8 Church Street, Wellington,
Telford, Shrops. TF1 1DG.
Tel. Telford 56272 (STD Code 0952)

72 High Street, Madeley,
Telford, Shrops. TF7 5AH.
Tel. Telford 585026 (STD Code 0952)

6 Oxford Street, Oakengates,
Telford, Shrops. TF2 6AA.
Tel. Telford 613536/7 (STD Code 0952)

14 Market Place, Shifnal, Shrops. TF11 9AZ.
Tel. Telford 461999 (STD Code 0952)

73 High Street, Newport, Shrops. TF10 7AU.
Tel. Newport 810882 (STD Code 0952)

4 Hazledine House, Central Square,
Telford Town Centre. TF3 4JL.
Tel. Telford 291722 (STD Code 0952)

Please reply to Madeley Office

VW.3107M

1st June, 1991

Mr. & Mrs. Brown,
Langholm Green,Madeley,
TELFORD,Shropshire.

Dear Mr. & Mrs. Brown,
re: Langholm Green, Madeley

Further to your recent communication with this office we note that you wish us to withdraw your above property from the market forthwith.

In accordance with our agency agreement signed and dated 25/2/91, we enclose herewith a note of our out-of-pocket expenses regarding this matter.

If we can be of any further help to you, please do not hesitate to contact us.

Yours sincerely,

D.B.ROBERTS & PARTNERS.

216 Brentwood
Brookside.
East Stourside.

Dear Mr Brown
   Amanda was absent because
she had a flu bug which was
running through the family
         Yours sincerely
         R. V. Hartfield

EAST STOURSIDE COUNCIL – EDUCATION DEPARTMENT

Date: 11th February 1991

Memorandum

To: All Course Organisers
From: Fiona Stanley
Subject: Courses at the Civic Hall,
              Westbridge.

Please note the attached memo, which refers to an e
organised by an Adviser at the Civic Hall.

Course members must be requested to return all cups and
saucers to the serving area and not take them into the
Hall itself. This will allow the catering staff to
complete their task of washing-up and clearing away.

Otherwise you will be called upon to do it
yourself!

EAST STOURSIDE
Council

ERNEST WOODS COMPREHENSIVE SCHOOL

-8 FEB 1991

Joan Hanna, Headteacher

Spencer Road, Herthington, East Stourside ES9 7TF. Tel: Stourside (0795) 060 6612

4th February 1991

CM/SRJ
Mr H R Jones, Management Services Officer
East Stourside, Hersey House
Whitstable Road, East Stourside ES8 7JJ

Dear Mr Jones
REGARDING 29th JANUARY, 1991

I am writing to express my annoyance at the manner in which the responsibility for 'dirty cups' was passed down to myself and the three pupils who provided the tea and coffee for the meeting on the morning of the above date.

I personally would NEVER have left a room or facility in a dirty condition after using it, nor would there have been cups left. I saw to it that all cups were collected from the Hall where coffee was served, and that all were washed, dried and put away. Confirmation of this could be gained from tea ladies preparing food for the Rotary Club at the same time as we were making coffee.

I personally returned after the telephone call, (which stated 80 cups had been left) to find 24 cups and saucers placed in the hall on a table. These were not there when I left at 11.45am. I can only assume then that people in the meeting took cups with them and did not return them to the Hall. I am not responsible for people who do this and then do not clear up afterwards. This is the responsibility of the person booking the room for the meeting.

Perhaps all persons arranging meetings in this room should be reminded that there is not a facility for tidying up after them and that they are responsible for the room being left in the same condition as they found it — including the washing of any cups remaining at the end.

Yours sincerely

E. G. Gordon

E.G. Gordon (Mrs)
Head of Department, Home Economics

Mrs Stanley Mrs Hamilton
Mr Meek   Mrs Goole

27 New Street,
Herthington,
East Stourside,
ES9 7SA.

Dear Matchrite,

I would like to complain about the way I was treated over an order I made some time ago. I ordered a selection of things from your catalogue, and got sent all but one of them (the missing one was a Joke Brick) with a credit note reading 'More in one week, please reorder', and £1.60 credit towards my next order. This meant I would have to pay for the postage and packing (and the stamps for the sending of the order form) again when I could have just waited a week longer for my order or have been given my money back for that item. Also, the catalogue I was sent with my order had a new price for the brick: £2.20, meaning even if I had used the credit note I would have still had to pay 60p to get the Joke Brick. You were not within your rights sending a credit note and I would like either £1.60 IN CASH back or the item I ordered.

Yours sincerely,

Robert Brown

Robert Brown

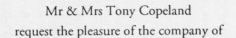

Mr & Mrs Tony Copeland
request the pleasure of the company of

Mr and Mrs Richard Brown

at the marriage of their daughter
EMMA MARY
with
MR. DAVID JOHN HENDERSON

at St Bartholomew's Church, Northcombe
on Saturday 11th April, 1992 at 2.30 pm
and afterwards at Northcombe Village Hall.

Home Farm, Bailey's Lane,
Northcombe, Loundshire
NB8 2DN

27 New Street, Herthington, East Stourside, ES9 7SA

29th January 1992

Mr and Mrs Richard Brown are pleased to accept Mr & Mrs Tony
Copeland's invitation to the marriage of their daughter, Emma Mary,
to Mr David John Henderson.

POSTBAG: YOU SAY

1

They're credit to NHS

I WOULD like to applaud the NHS. I was seen as an out patient at a consultant's clinic at the Queen Elizabeth Hospital, Gateshead, only five weeks after being referred there by my GP.

Then, on February 17, only three months after going on the waiting list, I was admitted to ward nine of the Queen Elizabeth Hospital for an operation.

The care and consideration given to me could not have been bettered. All the staff are a credit to the NHS and I am very grateful to all of them.

Thank you all, particularly Sister Allinson and all the staff of Ward 9, and to Mr Baker and his surgical team.

– A J HUTTON, Sheriff Hill
Newcastle Evening Chronicle

2

No classless society

THE letter from Billy Turnbull in the *Evening Chronicle* of Thursday, February 20, brought back memories of the Quayside.

I was young and poor. I remember you got a lovely coat for a shilling and a lovely dress for sixpence and lots of other things for only coppers. The people, then, only put the clothes in a pile on the ground and you picked out what you liked and gave the money to the salespeople.

Now, we are all better off and can manage. But I say, no matter who gets into Parliament, there will always be three classes of people, the rich, middle class and poor class. There always has been and always will be.

All we need in this world is a little love and kindness to make it a better world. It costs nothing to be kind to one another.

– NAME and address supplied.
Newcastle Evening Chronicle

> • **Please**
> • **keep**
> • **your**
> • **letters**
> • **brief**

3

Do stop moaning

WILL you please stop printing letters in your paper from the moaning pensioners of Newcastle about the 15p bus fares.

It has been going on for months and months and people are getting sick to death of hearing it. Why should they think they are different to other people?

In County Durham we pay £5 each April for our passes then half fare each time on the bus.

When my wife and I come into Newcastle it is 53p each way. If we go to Durham it is 60p each both ways, so I don't think people in Newcastle have anything to complain about.

Don't let's hear any more rubbish about free travel.

– E SCOTT, Ropery Lane, Chester-le-Street
Newcastle Evening Chronicle

5

Say NO to foxhunting

Dear Editor,

I AM writing to say that I totally agree with Esther Clarke (ET 207), foxhunting should be stopped.

The scientific evidence shows that the image of a fox as a pest is grossly exaggerated in anecdote and folklore. And if it were a pest, hunting would be an extremely inefficient and ineffective means of control.

Hunts kill less than three per cent of the fox population annually – inflicting pain, suffering and a bloody death on about 13,000 foxes a year, without making any real difference to the population as a whole.

Annette Day (ET 210) mentioned that if foxhunting were banned, a great number of foxhounds would have to be put down. This is not necessarily true, the hounds could still be used for drag hunting – chasing a trail laid by a human, and so all the good sport of riding to hounds would be preserved, without the cruelty to foxes of the hunt and kill.

Opinion polls show that the vast majority of people in Britain want an end to foxhunting. It's time to listen to the majority view.

– EMILY DEAN, 12, SHEFFIELD.
EARLY TIMES

4

STAR LETTER

DEATH SENTENCE?

Driving me crazy

Dear Editor,
I AM writing to complain about the term, 'joy-riding'. I think people should call it something like 'death-driving', because when people talk about it they think that joy is fun, so joy-riding is fun; which it isn't.

– BEN WESTAWAY, 10, KENT.
EARLY TIMES

6

Not the answer

Dear Editor,

I AM writing to disagree with James Duncan's letter in ET 210.

He said that teenagers who have committed crimes should go to prison. I think that this is one of the worst things that could happen. At least three young people have committed suicide in prison.

He said that caring for an elderly person was an unsuitable punishment. I also think this is true, however I don't think that prison is the answer. Even if they are put in prison, they should have a counsellor or someone to talk to about anything they're worried about.

Most teenagers who have committed serious crimes have had a bad childhood. Being put in prison could be the last straw!

– JENNIE DUNFORD, 13, LONDON.
EARLY TIMES

Dear Jo

7

Dear Jo

MY little brother gets lots of itchy red patches on his arms and legs and especially behind his knees. My mum says it is probably eczema and it will go away.

Only he scratches and makes it bleed and it looks disgusting. Can he do anything to get rid of it?

THE good news about eczema is that it does usually get better as you get older. But it can be a terrible nuisance for lots of young people.

Eczema is a skin condition which makes your skin itchy and red. Doctors don't really under-stand what causes eczema. It's a puzzling allergy-type condition in the same way that hay fever is. Both conditions tend to run in families but then not everyone in the family inherits them. You certainly can't catch eczema from other people. So you or your brother's friends won't get his eczema.

For the person who has eczema, it seems that their skin reacts when it comes into contact with certain things. Eczema sufferers should try to wear cotton clothes next to their skin. Wool and artificial fibres seem to irritate. So do some soaps, detergents and perfumes. Also some foods seem to make some people's eczema worse. If the eczema sufferer can recognise what they are, he or she can try to avoid eating them.

Some people find that their eczema gets worse with stress. So try to avoid getting into a flap and learn to talk to someone when you are worried or need help.

And ask your doctor if he or she has some cream to use on the eczema. It may help.

EARLY TIMES

8

Dear Jo

My friend is getting lots of ciga-rettes from her friend and she smokes them after school. She has had about five now. She is only 11 years old, so I want to tell her to stop because I think they look stupid, but I don't know how to tell her because it might hurt her feelings.

By now everyone must be aware that smoking is bad for your health. Just show her the printed warnings on the packets and adverts if she needs reminding.

Most young people start smoking because they think it looks grown up. Lots of grown-ups wish they could stop. I'm sure your friend can find healthier ways of looking grown- up.

EARLY TIMES

Dear Dr Pete

9

Dear Dr Pete,
Do men and women have the same number of ribs?
Michael Filliary, London.

Yes, I think a lot of people get confused about this because in the Bible it says that God took a rib from Adam and made Eve. There is also an odd fact about the human body which might also cause confusion.

Normally men and women do have 12 ribs each. That's 12 on each side of the body. You can feel them at the front and back of your own chest. Most of us are familiar with these from pictures of skeletons.

However, many people do have an extra rib. It's high up near the collar bone usually when it occurs. Some books say as many as one person in 20 has one (my anatomy and surgery books put it much lower at 0.5 per cent. That's one in 200). Anyway, it's probably somewhere between the two. Many people have one and never know because it doesn't ever bother them.

However, and this is the important part as far as this question goes, men seem to have an extra rib more often than women. It might be as much as three times more often. So in days past, when people read the Bible, and perhaps saw male skeletons with extra ribs on gallows and gibbets, they might have assumed falsely that all men have one more rib than women.

EARLY TIMES

10

Dear Dr Pete,
What causes glandular fever? I have it and it's taking ages to get better.
Emma Clarke, 14, Manchester.

Glandular fever is caused by a virus. It's an infectious disease, and mainly affects young people. Sometimes it's spread by kissing – and so is sometimes called the 'kissing disease'.

It takes much longer to get over than most viral infections like colds. You may feel rotten for some weeks yet. It's important to rest and eat well while you are getting better. One thing is certain – even though there is no cure for glandular fever yet – you will eventually get well.

EARLY TIMES

Some of the earliest novels in English were written as letters. The novelist, Samuel Richardson, began by trying to write a book of 'sample letters' for young ladies to copy. As he wrote he started to make these sample letters link up with one another, and he ended up by writing novels. One of his novels, Clarissa, *is the longest novel ever written in English. It was published in 1747, and it is written entirely in the form of letters. There are 537 letters written mostly between two pairs of people: the heroine, Clarissa, writes to her close friend Anna Howe, and the villain, Lovelace, writes to his close friend, Belford. This means that you often hear about the same incident from two different points of view.*

In his autobiography, Boy, *Roald Dahl gives the following account of writing letters at a boarding school in the 1920s.*

Letter-writing was a serious business at St Peter's. It was as much a lesson in spelling and punctuation as anything else because the Headmaster would patrol the classrooms all through the sessions, peering over our shoulders to read

> this is my Christmas wish list, as far as I can see.
> A mashie-niblick, (which I have to close).
> A decent book.
> I can't think of any thing else: if you send me a catalogue I might be able to tell you.

what we were writing and to point out our mistakes. But that, I am quite sure, was not the main reason for his interest. He was there to make sure that we said nothing horrid about his school.

There was no way, therefore, that we could ever complain to our parents about anything during term-time. If we thought the food was lousy or if we hated a certain master or if we had been thrashed for something we did not do, we never dared to say so in our letters. In fact, we often went the other way. In order to please that dangerous Headmaster who was leaning over our shoulders and reading what we had written, we would say splendid things about the school and how lovely the masters were.

> A man called Mr Nichell gave us a fine lecture last knight on birds, he told us how owls eat mice they eat the hole mouse skin and all, and then all the skin and bones goes into a sort of little parcel in side him and he puts it on the ground, and those are caled pelets and he showed us some pictures of some with he has faund, and of lotes of other Birds.

Mind you, the Headmaster was a clever fellow. He did not want our parents to think that those letters of ours were censored in this way, and therefore he never allowed us to correct a spelling mistake in the letter itself. If, for example, I had written... last Tuesday knight we had a lecture..., he would say:

'Don't you know how to spell night?'
'Y-yes, sir, k-n-i-g-h-t. '
'That's the other kind of knight, you idiot!'
'Which kind, sir? I... don't understand.'

'The one in shining armour! The man on horseback! How do you spell Tuesday night?'

'I'm not quite sure, sir. I... I...

'It's n-i-g-h-t, boy, n-i-g-h-t. Stay in and write it out for me fifty times this afternoon. No, no! Don't change it in the letter! You don't want to make it any messier than it is! It must go as you wrote it!'

Thus, the unsuspecting parents received in this subtle way the impression that your letter had never been seen or censored or corrected by anyone.

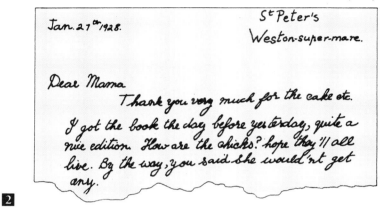

Anne Fine's novel *A Pack of Liars is about a series of letters between a class of children and their penpals. This is an extract from the first chapter.*

Look at this.

Oliver slid the letter across the desk and Laura picked it up. Although the spelling was correct, the handwriting was so frightful that Laura could barely read it in places.

> *17 Cat Alley*
> *Sticklebury*
> *10th October*
>
> *Dear Penpal*
> *I have been forced to write to you because I live in Sticklebury and your teacher needs one more penpal from our town to make enough go round your class.*
> *She happens to know my aunt, so my aunt forced me into writing this letter. I am taller than average. I bite my finger nails until they bleed. It drives them mad. I have huge feet. I get on people's nerves because I fidget and squirm and twitch all day. I'm always tapping my feet on the bars of people's chairs. It drives them mad but I can't help it. My mother says I've always been restless and even as a baby I never wanted to be held and had to struggle all the time. I can't get to sleep at nights and lie there thinking extremely dark thoughts. I haven't any real friends my own age. but I get on with the boy next door—he's going to be three next week. I have this pebble I found, and I can't stop fingering it. It drives them mad.*

And I have this problem. There's only a few of the stairs that I can tread on. I can't put my feet down on the ones which have the yellow swirly bit of pattern. And the same goes for the assembly hall at school. I can't tread on some of the tiles, so I walk all funny when I'm in there. It drives them mad. And I can't take anything at all out of my school locker if I've touched the sides with my hand first — even if I just brush the edge the slightest bit, accidentally. So I get into trouble because I've never got the right things for gym or football. It drives them mad.

There are even worse things, but they are private.
How are you? I hope you are quite well.
Yours sincerely,
Simon Hugget

When she had finished reading the letter, Laura flattened it out on her desk top and stared at it a little apprehensively.

'Well?' Oliver's plastic spectacle frames slipped down to the end of his nose. He tipped his head back to peer at Laura through the lenses. 'What do you think?'

'Perhaps it's a joke.'

'Of course it's not a joke.' Oliver dashed the suggestion.

'No,' Laura admitted. 'It sounds real.'

She picked the letter off the desk and flicked it between her fingers.

'Just your luck, Oliver,' she commiserated. 'Twenty-one Sticklebury penpals, and you have to get the local nutter.'

'I beg your pardon?'

Oliver's tone was cool.

'Well,' Laura said. 'He can't be normal, can he? He's obviously wacko. Unhinged. A total basket case.'

Oliver was outraged.

'Wacko?' he said. 'Unhinged? A basket case? What do you mean? He might be a little bit nervy by nature. Even a trace over-active, perhaps. But he's perfectly normal.'

'Perfectly normal?' Laura stared at Oliver in amazement. 'You must be mad!'

Oliver stared back.

'I can see,' he said coldly, 'that round here it's getting so you're considered a nut case if you don't share the same small habits and views as your neighbour!'

Then, inasmuch as it is possible whilst sitting in a double desk to turn one's back, Oliver did so.

Laura wasn't bothered. Although his waspish tongue had terrified her at the start, over the two terms she had been sitting next to Oliver Boot Laura had become accustomed to him. Ignoring his stern withdrawal, she turned her attention to the first letter from her own new penpal.

2D Cathedral Close
Sticklebury

Dear Friend
*Would you like to write to me? I would like that. It would be nice. I hope you
will. How are you? I hope you are well.*

Laura stifled a yawn.

*Where do you live? Are there a lot of houses on your street? There are a lot of
houses on my street. What is your house like? How many rooms do you have?
Do you have lots of neighbours like we do?*

Laura shook her head in amazement. She had never read such a boring
letter in her whole life.

*Do you have any pets? I have no pets. Do you have a colour television? We do.
Do you have a video? We do. Ours is new. Is yours new? We have four radio-
cassette players in our house. How many do you have? We have a stereo
system, too. Do you have a stereo system? We have a computer. Do you?*

Here, Laura turned towards Oliver and tapped him gently on the shoulder.
'Oliver,' she said. 'I want to say I'm very sorry that I said what I did about
your new penpal. He clearly isn't barmy at all.'
Appeased, Oliver shifted round in the double seat.
'Mine is, though,' Laura added.
Behind his spectacles, Oliver raised his eyes to heaven.
'Laura,' he said. 'The whole point of having a penpal is to widen your
horizons. If you go round thinking other people are barmy just because they
are a little bit different from you – '
'Read this, please, Oliver,' Laura interrupted.
Oliver furrowed his brows to read the letter. He was a quick reader, even if
he did still move his lips a little. He had soon read as far as Laura.

*We have a computer. Do you have a computer? What sort is it? We have some
electric hedge shears. Do you have any electric hedge shears? We keep ours in
the garden shed. Where do you keep yours? We have a microwave oven. Do
you?*

> *With best wishes,*
> *Your penpal,*
> *Philip*

Oliver was silent – for him, a quite rare occurrence.
'Well?' Laura prompted. 'What do you think?'
'I think,' declared Oliver. 'That you should ask Mrs Coverley if you can
swap penpals with someone else.'

What to look for

You may find some of the following ideas helpful when you are discussing the letters:

Letters in our society

Letters are extremely important in our society. We use them to keep in touch with friends, to give and receive information, to communicate with banks, building societies and insurance companies, to make requests, and to make complaints. The Post Office delivers 60 million letters every day, or one letter for every woman, child and man in the country. Homes, schools, hospitals, charities, sports clubs and businesses all rely on letters.

Purpose

Letters can be written for all sorts of different purposes – to inform, to find out, to complain, to entertain, to thank, to keep in touch, to remind, and for many other reasons. The purpose of any letter should have a strong influence on the way in which it is written. If the purpose of a letter is not clear, it may be a waste of time writing it.

Tone

The tone of a letter will depend on who is being written to, what is being written about, and how the writer feels about the subject of the letter. The tone might be:

> **formal**
> *for example, a letter to a bank*
> **chatty**
> *a letter to a close friend*
> **cold**
> *a letter of complaint*
> **angry**
> *a letter to a newspaper*
> **solemn**
> *a letter of condolence.*

What other examples can you give?

The tone of a letter can sometimes be seen in the layout; a formal letter is more likely to have a standard layout and a formal greeting, such as 'Dear Sir or Madam', rather than 'Hi Jane'. It is also more likely to be typed or word-processed, and to be written or printed on headed paper.

Layout

The layout of letters varies a lot, as you will see from the letters displayed here, and from the letters you collect. A number of elements come up in most letters, although they may be shown in different ways and in different places. For example:

writer's address
this may well be in the form of a printed letterhead

logo
companies often use special designs to help make the name of their company seem special

receiver's address
common on more formal letters – useful for keeping records

date
almost always given

reference
common on more formal letters – it helps with filing copies of the letter

greeting
almost always given, but the greeting chosen will depend on how formal the letter is

heading
common on more formal letters – it helps the reader to know at once what the letter is going to be about

content
usually in a series of paragraphs, which may be quite short

parting
almost always given, but the parting chosen will depend on how formal the letter is

postscript
usually something that has been forgotten, but a postscript may well be something that has been deliberately placed at the end for extra emphasis.

Relationship between writer and receiver

If you wrote a letter to a friend, it would probably be informal and chatty, because you know each other well, you are equals, and you like each other. If you were to write to the Queen, however, your letter would be very formal, because you do not know each other, and are not socially equal. If the Queen wrote to you, she could be less formal than you would be with her. However, if the Queen and Prince Philip wrote to each other, they might be as informal and chatty as you might be with your friend.

The table below shows some of the patterns you might expect:

Relationship	Letter likely to be...
close	informal – subject may be personal
distant	more formal – subject less likely to be personal
friendly	informal
unfriendly	more formal
equal	informal
unequal	more formal
financial	formal and detailed
official	very formal
personal	informal

Technology

Many personal letters are still written by hand, but most business letters are now either typed or word-processed. Computers make it possible for companies to send many more letters much more cheaply. Many companies use a computer process called mail merging. In this process, a file containing a list of names and addresses is 'merged' with a file containing a standard letter. The computer then prints each letter with a different name and address. Mail merging is very commonly used for 'junk mail' (see Letter A in the anthology). Some people prefer to have a letter that is handwritten. Signatures are almost always handwritten, but the person's name may be typed as well. Some people will add a handwritten line or two to make a typed letter seem more personal. With a word-processed letter, you should never need to have a PS (a postscript), but people still use them.

General activities

1 Letters in our society

Work with a small group to collect as many different letters as you can.

a Sort all the letters into different types. Look closely at the letters before you decide what the types will be.

b Look at the letters in each of the groups you have sorted. What do they have in common?

You could consider:
purpose
tone
layout
writer
receiver
relationship between writer and receiver
subject
technology used.

2 Letters in our society

Work with a small group to conduct a survey of pupils in your class:

- *When did they last write a letter?*
- *To whom?*
- *For what purpose?*
- *How often do they write letters?*
- *How do they feel about writing letters?*
- *Who do they receive letters from?*
- *How often do they receive letters?*
- *How do they feel about the letters they receive?*

Plan how you will present your findings – as a report or as a display? You could explore whether there are differences between girls and boys, or between older and younger pupils.

3 Letters in our society

Conduct the survey suggested in activity 2, but ask the questions of adults. Try to choose adults with a range of different jobs, for example, a teacher, a full-time parent, a shop assistant, and a secretary. Compare your results with someone who has carried out the same survey amongst pupils.

4 Letters in our society

Keep a record of all the letters that come into and go out of your home over the period of a fortnight. For each letter, keep a note of when it arrived (or when it was sent), who it was from, who it was to, and what it was about. Many of the letters will be private, but you may be able to use some of them to put together a display of a fortnight's mail.

5 Exploring purposes

Work with a friend to 'brainstorm' as many purposes for writing letters as you can think of. Use coloured pencils to highlight your list, for example, one colour for the purposes of letters that you have written yourself, and another colour for the purposes of letters that you (or your family) have received.

Try to collect at least one example of all the different purposes of letter you have suggested, and ask your teachers and others in your class to collect examples for you. Such a collection of letters could be made into a wall display, or they could be collected together in a scrapbook.

6 Exploring tone

Work with a friend to choose three or four letters which you think have contrasting tones. (It would be better to collect letters of your own, but if you are choosing from the anthology in this book, you might try letters C, D, I and J.) Try to explain to each other exactly what the tone of each letter is, and which features of the language or layout give it this tone. Use pens or coloured pencils to mark up a copy of each letter to show which words or expressions contribute to its overall tone. In each case, explain why you think the writer has chosen this particular tone for this purpose and this audience. Display the highlighted letters on a large sheet of sugar paper.

7 Exploring layout

Work with a friend to choose three or four letters which have very different layouts. (It would be better to collect letters of your own, but if you are choosing from this book, try letters B, F, G and H.) Use pens or colours to circle or highlight all the different elements of the layout in each letter. In some cases you may wish to indicate elements which are not in a letter. What are the differences between the letters? Can you explain these differences by considering the various purposes, writers, and receivers of each letter?

8 Exploring layout

Work with a friend to collect as many varied letters as you can. Cut them up so that you have a pile of writers' addresses, a pile of greetings, a pile of dates, and so on. When you cut up the letters, try to make sure that you keep a sense of the overall layout of the letter, such as the position of the date on the right or on the left. Select as many contrasting examples as you can from each pile, and paste them up so that you have a sheet of greetings, a sheet of dates, and so on. Highlight the differences between the examples on each sheet.

9 Exploring relationships

Collect as many letters as you can which show different relationships. How are the relationships shown in the language, the layout and the content of the letters?

10 Exploring technologies

Find as many examples as you can of different technologies in the letters you have collected. Look for evidence of word-processing, mail merging, typing, printing, photocopying, other copying, faxing, electronic mail, handwriting, simulated handwriting, and so on.

Activities to focus on specific letters

Junk mail

EXPLORATION
- *What is the tone of the letter?*
- *What is the purpose of the letter?*
- *What is the relationship between the writer and the receiver?*
- *Is this a good letter? Could it be improved?*

LOOK AT:

Technology The letter is clearly word-processed, but why has the company chosen to use such a poor-quality printer?

Date Why isn't there one?

Organisation Why is there a PS? (With a word processor you shouldn't need a PS. Can you explain why?)

Capital letters Why have some words been printed in block capitals?

EXPLORATION

'Junk mail' letters like this one are often extremely cleverly written.

Look closely at this letter and think about how it is trying to persuade the receiver. For example:

- *How does it try to make the receiver feel that he or she is special?*
- *How does it try to make sure that the main junk mail shot isn't just thrown away?*
- *How does it try to make it seem that the receiver is almost certain to win a prize?*
- *Is that the Prize Draw Manager's real name?*
- *How many other people do you think will have received a similar letter?*
- *How do you think the company decides who to write to?*

ACTIVITY 1

Have you or your parents received letters like this? Do you read them? Find out from your teacher and from others in your class what they do with their junk mail.

ACTIVITY 2

Collect as many examples of junk mail as you can from other pupils in the class. Study them carefully. What features do they have in common? Can you find two letters which appear to be from different companies but which are clearly written by the same person? If you look at a whole envelope of junk mail, you will find that there may be a whole series of different messages written by a series of different people. There may be a variety of different typefaces, and a variety of types of production – colour printing, word-processing, handwriting, and so on. Try displaying all the contents of one junk mail envelope on a large sheet of sugar paper. Then use a large pen to highlight and comment on the different purposes, writers, readers, technologies and layouts that are being used.

ACTIVITY 3

Write the letter that the company would send to the prize draw winner.

ACTIVITY 4

Work with a group to produce your own junk mail shot advertising your school **or** work on a computer to produce mail merge letters for everyone in your class.

Holiday company

EXPLORATION

- *What is the tone of the letter?*
- *What is the purpose of the letter?*
- *What is the relationship between the writer and the receiver?*
- *Is this a good letter? Could it be improved?*

How can you tell?

Look particularly at the logo, at the greeting, and at the parting. Where else would you find letters of this kind? Can you collect any examples that are similar?

ACTIVITY 1

Some features of the letter suggest that it was not written by a native speaker of English. Make a note of these, and compare your notes with a friend's.

Redraft the letter so that it reads more naturally. Is your version as welcoming as the original?

ACTIVITY 2

If you have ever been on holiday to another country, you will probably have come across examples of letters, notices or instructions written in English by speakers of other languages. See how many of these you can collect. Could you write similar letters or notices in their languages? Try translating announcements and letters from your school noticeboard into another language.

Insurance company

EXPLORATION

- *What is the tone of the letter?*
- *What is the purpose of the letter?*
- *What is the relationship between the writer and the receiver?*
- *What does the letter tell you about the company?*
- *Is this a good letter? Could it be improved?*

How can you tell?

LOOK AT:

Layout	**The use of paper with places marked for the address, date and reference. The heading.**
The greeting	**Why has such a formal greeting been chosen? What is the effect of using Sirs rather than Sir?**
The writer	**Who is 'we'?**
Vocabulary	**What kinds of words are used?**
Spelling	**What can we learn from the spelling mistake?**
Signature	**Can you read it?**

ACTIVITY 1

Can you find any other letters like this one? What are the advantages and disadvantages of marking places for the address, date, reference and so on?

Thank you letter

EXPLORATION

- *What is the tone of the letter?*
- *What is the purpose of the letter?*
- *What is the relationship between the writer and the receivers?*
- *Is this a good letter? Could it be improved?*

How can you tell?

LOOK AT:

Content	What sort of things are mentioned? Which things are not mentioned? What does the writer assume that the readers already know?
Organisation	How does the letter start and finish?
Presentation	Handwriting, corrections.

ACTIVITY 1

You will probably have had to write thank you letters to friends or relatives after Christmas or your birthday. What did you do if you really didn't like the present that was sent? What do you write if your aunt and uncle have sent you exactly the same dull present two years in succession? Work with a group to prepare a list of rules for writing thank you letters which tell people what they should include in their thank you letters, and which give them advice on how to cope with the tricky ones.

ACTIVITY 2

Ask your teacher to show you how mail merging works on a school computer so that you can produce a thank you letter. Think carefully about how you can make your standard letter seem really personal.

School open letter

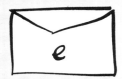

EXPLORATION:

- *What is the tone of the letter?*
- *What is the purpose of the letter?*
- *What is the relationship between the writer and the receiver?*
- *Is this a good letter? How might it be improved?*

How can you tell?

LOOK AT:

Layout	Why does it use headings?
Technology	How has it been produced?
Illustrations	Why do you think Robert has drawn on the letter?
Content	What sorts of things are mentioned? What sorts of things are not mentioned?
Delivery	How will the letter be sent? What are its chances of reaching its destination safely?

ACTIVITY 1

Does your school send out letters like this? Compare one of the letters from your own school with this one. Do a survey in your class to find out what percentage of these letters reach home safely.

Estate agent

EXPLORATION

- *What is the tone of the letter?*
- *What is the purpose of the letter?*
- *What is the relationship between the writer and the receivers?*
- *Is this a good letter? Could it be improved?*

How can you tell?

LOOK AT:

Layout Why are there so many addresses? What about the heading and the reference?

Words chosen Who chose them?

Signature Why do you think the letter was never signed?

ACTIVITY 1

Imagine that the estate agent has to write an equivalent letter to a client who is also a close friend. Have a go at rewriting this letter in a much more personal style.

Absence note

EXPLORATION

- *What is the tone of the letter?*
- *What is the purpose of the letter?*
- *What is the relationship between the writer and the receiver?*
- *Is this a good letter? Could it be improved?*

How can you tell?

LOOK AT:

Content What information is given?

Presentation What kind of paper is used?

Signature Can you read it?

ACTIVITY 1

Collect as many examples of absence notes as you can. How much do they vary? Which do you think are the most effective? Write some guidelines for parents sending absence notes.

Memo and complaint

EXPLORATION

- *What is the tone of each letter?*
- *What is the purpose of each letter?*
- *What is the relationship between the writers and the receivers?*
- *Are these good letters? Could they be improved?*

> *How can you tell?*

LOOK AT:

Technology What is pre-printed, what is typed, what is handwritten, and what is word-processed?

Organisation How do the letters start and finish? What is dealt with in each paragraph?

ACTIVITY 1

What is a memorandum? How is it different from an ordinary letter? How many examples of different memos can you collect?

ACTIVITY 2

How could you improve this letter of complaint? Write your own version of it.

ACTIVITY 3

Collect as many letters of complaint as you can. How clearly do they each state their case?

Write a reply to one of the letters you have collected, or write a letter of complaint of your own, especially if there is something that you actually want to complain about.

Letter of complaint

EXPLORATION

- *What is the tone of the letter?*
- *What is the purpose of the letter?*
- *What is the relationship between the writer and the receiver?*
- *Is this a good letter? Could it be improved?*

> *How can you tell?*

ACTIVITY 1

Write a reply to this letter.

ACTIVITY 2

Collect as many letters of complaint as you can. How clearly do they each state their case?

Write a reply to one of the letters you have collected, or write a letter of complaint of your own, especially if there is something that you actually want to complain about.

Wedding invitation and reply

This wedding invitation was received from Aunt Anne, who wrote the thank you letter (letter D).

EXPLORATION

- *What is the tone of the invitation and reply?*
- *What are the purposes of the letters?*
- *What is the relationship between the writers and the receivers?*
- *Are these good letters? Could they be improved?*

How can you tell?

ACTIVITY 1

Contrast these letters with the thank you letter (letter D). The people involved are the same, but the tone of the letters is very different. Why should this be?

ACTIVITY 2

Make your own collection of invitations and replies. These might be invitations to weddings, christenings, funerals, birthday parties, jumble sales, dinner parties or performances. What features do they have in common? What are their differences?

Letters to newspapers

EXPLORATION

Compare the range of subjects covered by the letters from the local newspaper with the range of subjects covered by the letters from the children's newspaper. Do the children and adults seem to have the same interests and concerns? How would you explain any differences? Do you think that the children's letters were all written by children?

Several of the letters refer to other letters, or to articles from the paper. Why do you think this is?

Look at the headlines used for the letters. These were written by the sub-editor at the newspaper, and not by the writers of the letters. Are the headlines helpful? Why do you think they were chosen? Can you suggest alternative headlines? What would it be like if no headlines were used?

Compare the letters from the problem page with the other letters from the same newspaper. How are they different? What differences are there between the letters to Dr Pete and the letters to Jo? How helpful do you find the answers?

People write to newspapers and magazines for a variety of different purposes – perhaps to air their opinions, to reply to a previous letter, to express their anger, or to exchange ideas and information. Try to identify the writer's purpose(s) in each of the letters on pages 18 – 20. Is the range of purposes the same for the adults' letters and the children's letters?

ACTIVITY 1

Find the letters page in one of the magazines or newspapers that you, your friends or your parents read. How does it compare with the letters shown here? Look at the range of subjects, and at the range of reasons for writing. How would you account for any differences?

ACTIVITY 2

Work with a group to collect letters pages from as wide a variety of newspapers and magazines as you can. For each newspaper or magazine, consider the following:

- *How many letters are there?*
- *How much space is given to letters?*
- *Make a list of all the different subjects raised.*
- *How often is each subject raised?*
- *How long are the longest and shortest letters?*
- *What is the average length of the letters?*
- *What purposes do the writers have?*
- *What kind of headings are the letters given?*

ACTIVITY 3

Write your own letter to a newspaper or magazine about an issue which concerns you.

ACTIVITY 4

Cut the problem pages out of a newspaper or magazine without reading the letters or the answers. Cut the answers off so that they are separate from the letters, and store them carefully. Work with a group to write your own answers to the problems given in the letters. Compare your answers with the originals.

ACTIVITY 5

Prepare an advertisement for your own problem page. Ask pupils from another class in your own school, or from a class in a neighbouring school, to send you letters. Write and publish the replies.

ACTIVITY 6

Write a letter of your own to send to a problem page. Send the letter to several different magazines. Compare any different replies that you receive.

Letters in stories and novels

ACTIVITY 1

What do you think are the advantages and disadvantages of writing a story through letters? Make a list of them. Have a go at writing your own story entirely through letters.

ACTIVITY 2

Do you think that the headteacher in *Boy* was right to read the boys' letters in the way that he did? What reasons might he give to justify doing it? Act out a scene in which the headteacher talks to the boys about letter–writing.

ACTIVITY 3

Imagine that you are a pupil at a school like St Peter's. Write a couple of letters that you might send to your parents, and write the extracts from your secret diary which tell the real story. You might go on to tell (or act out) the story of what happens when your secret diary is discovered.

ACTIVITY 4

Write replies to the two letters from *A Pack of Liars*.

ACTIVITY 5

Have you or your friends ever had penpals? Were the letters you received anything like the ones from *A Pack of Liars*? Talk together about which qualities you think a really good penpal would have.

ACTIVITY 6

Your English teacher or your modern languages teacher may be able to help you to find a penpal if you want one. They will probably be quite willing to help you with your letters, and to give you time to work on them during your lessons. Ask and see.

ACTIVITY 7

Work with a group to write a story that is based on the letters between two penpals living in different countries. Use reference books in the library to find out about the different countries so that you can make your letters as authentic as possible.